FR   R LOVED ONES IN HEAVEN

"We Are Still With You"

An Inspirational and Supportive Guide for Dealing with the Loss of a Loved One and Connecting with Them

BY

GUY DUSSEAULT

Guy Dusseault
Biddeford, Maine
info@oursonbilly.com
www.oursonbilly.com
Facebook – Signs From Our Loved Ones

Table of Contents

Introduction

This book came about from the nearly twelve years of learning about grieving the loss/crossing over of a loved one, what we all go through, and searching for answers.

For my family, it was losing our son, Billy, on June 26, 2004. Besides trying to survive the heartbreaking loss of Billy, we were also experiencing the sheer shock and unfathomable pain of the death, I was also thinking "Am I the only one going through this? Is there something wrong with me? Am I going crazy?"

No, we go through a grieving period and we are not alone with all we are going through during this time. It is a normal part of our grieving process. We mourn deeply because we love so intensely and that's okay.

We must heal at our own pace, which is usually small steps, one day at a time. Yet, I needed more. Yes, I needed to survive and breathe and exist every day without Billy, but I desperately wanted to find a way to connect with him, I had no idea if this was possible, but I had to try.

This book is a collection of my own experiences, as well as things I have learned from others and my research.

Following the loss of Billy, there were so many questions swirling around in my mind. It took me years of searching and reading, researching and asking countless questions. I gained so much knowledge from the sharing of experiences from others and from our own Facebook group pages *Signs from Our Loved Ones* and *Signs From Our Loved One−2*. I owe many "thank yous" to so many individuals who have helped me and my family and shared their experiences and knowledge with me.

Thank you and God Bless.

CHAPTER 1
Our Story

I would like to begin by sharing how I arrived where I am today after the loss/crossing over of our son, Billy, on June 26, 2004. He was twenty−eight years old and died only four days before his 29th birthday.

Saturday, June 26, 2004, our day began with a family get−together and barbecue at our home. Billy was one of the first one to arrive. We all had a great time being with our family and friends, some using our pool on this beautiful day and others playing games.

The last photo of Billy taken at our home that day in June when he passed away.

Billy had to leave late in the afternoon to get ready for a camp out at some friend's house that evening. Before he left our home, I helped him load up his truck with some items my wife gave him, like dishes and so forth. We talked a bit and said good−bye. I watched him leave our driveway.

A short time later, as Billy was headed to the camp out with his friends, he drove by the house and beeped his horn. Little did we realize that was going to be the last time we were going to be with, see, or hear from our son.

In the meantime, we continued with our family get together right into the evening with a small campfire in the yard to relax around. Our other son, Robert, went to join Billy at the friend's camp out. Robert was excited because the group was going to go four—wheeling on ATVs that evening.

My wife and I called it a night at around 10:30 p.m. or so. It wasn't long into my sleep when I had a dream that someone in our family had died. In my dream, I could see people gathering for the funeral, but I could not see who they were grieving over.

I awakened nearly in tears. The dream felt so real and emotional I thought about waking up my wife so we could call Billy and Robert to make sure they were okay, but I decided not to and shook off the experiences as a bad dream and nothing more.

The next morning, the dream was very much on my mind, but I never said anything to Jo—Anne and simply went about my day, as usual. However, I was quite down over the experience of my dream.

We were to meet other family members for breakfast. My sister, Ann, was leaving for her home in Georgia. We had breakfast on a closed—in glass patio. I was seated right by the window thinking about the dream and feeling depressed as I tried to make sense of it. Suddenly, this small sparrow came right up to the glass by my feet and stayed there for a while. I thought nothing of it at the time.

We had a wonderful time at breakfast and then soon left for my parents' place to say our good-bye to my sister, Ann. As we were talking, my other sister, June, walked in and gave us the news.

"One of our cousins was killed last night while at a camp out riding an ATV at night," June announce.

My knees then buckled and this overwhelming pain and fear came over me. Jo-Anne seemed to have the same reaction as we knew both of our sons were at a camp out with ATVs.

We all scrambled around to make some calls to see what exactly had happened and who had been killed. We were so scared and nervous. At first, we could not remember any phone numbers. We finally managed to recall the phone numbers and kept trying to get a hold of Billy and Robert to no avail.

Jo-Anne was able to reach one of the boys' friends, Kevin who gave the heartbreaking news.

"Billy was killed riding his ATV."

I was so angry. I slammed my parents' phone so hard that I broke it. The dream I'd had only hours earlier was a dream preparing me for that Sunday morning at 10:00 a.m. It was Billy sending me a message to help with what was to occur a few hours later.

Hearing that one of your children has just died is something you never expect or ever want to experience. I was in so much pain and shock I screamed and started to run down the hallway of my parents' high rise building and kept going until my sister and sister—in—law caught up to me.

To me, it seemed impossible for Billy to have died before us. It's not supposed to happen to any parent. This option was something that never even crossed my mind.

We all gathered outside my parents' building trying to figure out what to do next. It was like a living nightmare, but it was real. Our cousin, Rick, works for the Biddeford fire department down the street, so we headed there to see if we could get any more information. Rick made a phone call and confirmed it was indeed Billy who was killed last night while riding his ATV. The verification from an authority figure simply crushed our hearts and deepened our pain and heartbreak. It really was Billy who had lost his life mere hours ago.

We had to wait another three hours before we could go see his body. The ride home felt extremely long and all we wanted to do was to be with our other son, Robert.

As we arrived home, there were already a number of people there waiting to see us. We got out of the car and met Robert. The three of us hugged and cried. Nothing else seemed to matter at the time. We were also comforted by many family and friends, but all I wanted to do was sit on our back steps and shut everything out.

There wasn't anything anyone could say or do that would bring back our son, so I really wanted to be left alone.

There are no words which can accurately describe the feeling a parent goes through with the loss/crossing over of a beloved child. All you experience is the heartbreaking pain crushing of our heart and causing numbness. Unless you have been through it yourself, you cannot understand the agony.

Three hours later, we rode with my brother, sister—in—law, and parents to the Springvale Funeral Home to visit Billy's body. Even though I knew in my heart he was no longer with us, I had to see his body. Robert did not want to go. He wanted to remember Billy the way he was. When we arrived, we were led into a room. We asked if my wife and I could see Billy alone. My first reaction was to pick him up and bring him home or maybe… somehow he would wake up and be fine. However, that was not to be.

My wife would not leave his side. She stood by him rubbing his face and giving him a kiss. We both put our hands on Billy as we cried and talked to him. As I stared at him, it finally sunk in he was no longer here with us in the physical form.

It felt like the world had come crashing down around me. I remember in the few days after Billy's crossing over that I was so angry and I wanted to destroy things to release the negative energy I had inside of me. I paced all over our backyard wanting to hit something. I wanted to visit the place where Billy had his accident, but my family would not tell me where it had happened. I was not in any condition to drive, so I had to wait.

About three days after Billy crossed over, my brother, Peter, brought me to the scene of the accident which caused so many emotions and tears. Because of all the anger I had inside, I brought a metal baseball bat with me and I used it on the tree and rock where Billy crashed. I swung the bat with everything I had in me until the it finally broke apart. Even though my hands hurt from the vibrations of the bat, it felt so good. However brief the release was, it helped me face my anger and negative feelings that were inside of me. My brother told me I made wailing sound while hitting the tree, but it's not something I remember. I no longer had any feeling of wanting to destroy things or much anger left in me.

It had only been a few days. I was still in shock and hoping and waiting to see Billy walk through our door, even though I knew it was impossible. Deep down, I was always wishing it would happen.

I was so depressed I didn't want to do much of anything at all. Over the next few months, I lost about thirty-five pounds. It was hard for me to eat. It took me six weeks before I could go back to work. Even then, it was only part time and I would break down on the job site so much that when I did go to work, I would park my truck behind buildings or trees so I would have a place to get away from everything. I don't believe I said more than a handle full of words to others while I was at work. I mostly wanted to go home and be with my wife. There were many nights Jo-Anne and I would simply hold each other and cry until we fell asleep.

I do have to say we have a great family and wonderful friends who would always check up on us, bring food, and, most importantly, just be there. Most of the time, we would all sit there watching TV or talking to each other. It wasn't about what we were doing; it was about the company and the support. Those folks could never understand how much it meant to us because it's not easy to visit someone who has lost a loved one. However, their support meant the world to us.

For most people who have dealt with the loss/crossing over of a loved one as we have, we love to hear when others share stories about their own loved ones and to mention their name. It hurts more when others avoid the subject altogether. In sharing their stories, it keeps them a part of us with a bond of love that can never be broken.

It didn't take long for me to start looking into if there was any way possible for me to find a way to connect with Billy. As time passed, I read books, searched the internet, and studied many websites looking for anything to do with connecting with a loved one who had crossed over. I gathered a lot of information to help me along, but I was unable to connect right away with Billy or see the signs he might send to let us know he was okay and still around us.

My grief and depression were too deep to make any connection on my own or see any signs.

After seven months, Jo–Anne was talking to someone who had lost her daughter in a car wreck only a short distance from where our son had had his accident. They also struggled especially since the woman's husband was losing weight like I had, as well. The woman made an appointment with a medium named Vicki Monroe (www.vickimonroe.com) who then helped them connect with their daughter on the other side. This helped them tremendously in their healing process. She mentioned this to my wife thinking this might be of some help to us.

Jo–Anne asked, "Would you be interested in going for a reading?"

I replied, "Absolutely I would!"

This seemed like my last hope to make contact with Billy which I wanted to do more than anything.

My wife called Vicki and made an appointment for us set for February 16, 2005, at 10:00 a.m. We had to wait for over two weeks to meet Vicki and to make a connection with Billy. It felt like it took forever for the two weeks to go by. We had never had a reading before nor did we know what to expect since we had never been to a medium.

When the morning of February 16th came, I remember being so nervous. Since I was struggling so much with the loss, I felt if Billy didn't come through, I would be extremely disappointed and may never get over my depressed or escape its grip on me.

Before we left, I went into the bathroom and prayed, asking Billy to please come through and let us know he was okay.

We arrived for the reading with Vicki Monroe and she made us feel right at home. It was like meeting a friend you have known for a long time which helped us not be so nervous. The reading was amazing and the details she gave us were things no one could ever have known except for us. The messages helped bring some great comfort to us.

Here's an example of a message Billy gave us through Vicki that my wife did not even know about:

Because I was so depressed, I had lost about thirty-five pounds. A couple of times when I'd walk out of the shower, I'd looked in the mirror and say to myself, *"If anyone walked into the bathroom right now, all they would see is water hitting the floor. They wouldn't even be able to see me because I've lost some much weight. I would be invisible."*

I had not told one single person about this. I hadn't even said it out loud; only in my mind. Vicki Monroe relayed the same message to me, only I knew it was from Billy to us. He had heard my thoughts.

Meeting Vicki Monroe was the first in a number of steps in our healing. Healing doesn't happen overnight. There's no magic pill.

And, for most people, it takes a number of events in our lives to help us heal. The process is different for everyone. You take it one very small step and one day at a time at your own pace and done your way.

We will never "get over" the loss/crossing over of our loved ones. We simply do the best we can in our own way and know we are not alone or going crazy. We are grieving… a moment, minute, hour, or day at a time.

CHAPTER 2
My New Journey

After our reading with Vicki Monroe, I continued to read as much as I could to learn more and to find a way to receive signs from Billy.

While researching, I learned one of the ways our loved ones are able to connect with us is through photos by using their energy to get our attention and demonstrate they are still around us. This is what many call "orbs" although it's better referred to as spirit energy, ectoplasm, or another form of spirit energy. It's a symbol of our loved one's constant and unconditional love. To view some of the amazing photographs, visit our website at www.oursonbilly.com for a number of beautiful spirit energy photos of different types including our favorite, the heart—shaped images of the moon and light.

After learning about this form of spirit energy, I thought I should give it a try to see what I could discover. I used my wife's Kodak Easy Share 3.2 megapixel camera in April 2005. I went out into our back yard and randomly started taking pictures in different directions with nothing in particular to photograph. When taking a few photos, I looked at the viewer to see if there were any orbs or spirit energy captured, but the screen was too small to see anything at all. I went back into the house and to my office. I took out the memory card and inserted it into my computer to download and have a closer look. To my surprise, sure enough, I had a number of amazing photographs of orbs or spirit energy in my pictures.

I began taking photos daily; in the morning, afternoon, and evening. I was able to have many spirit energy images show up daily giving me beautiful signs from Billy and others letting us know they were around us.

Not only can our loved ones get our attention in this form, but so can our spirit guides. We all have spirit guides who help and watch over us and our loved ones. There are also angels, fairies, ascended masters, and pets all with unconditional love. They're all able to use their energy to show up as orbs or spirit energy to let us know they are still around us and always full of love.

I kept taking hundreds of photos nearly every day and logging them into my photos files. Then, one day in July 2005, after we returned from the movies, I decide to take a few photos. That is the night I knew being able to take these photos had to be more than just for me to photograph. I started taking snapping away and could not believe how many spirit energies were around me. It looked like a snow storm on this warm July evening. I must have taken around three hundred or so photos that night. I would have taken more, but the memory cards back then could not hold as many as the ones can today.

From that day on, I continue to take these types of pictures.

A few months later, in late October, I was reviewing photos from a week or so earlier. I noticed one of my photos seemed like it had a misty look to it in the shape of a heart. I learned this is another way for our loved ones, spirit guides, angels, and more, to use their energy. Just like the orbs, it is different form of spirit energy they are able to use to get our attention and are around us, always with love.

Visit our website www.oursonbilly.com to see more of these photos.

I have taken many photos in the past and never noticed the orbs or spirit energy until now. Even more, in this one photo, I noted the moon looked different. It was in a perfect heart shape, as well.

I learned that our loved ones are able to manipulate light by using their energy to shape it into different forms, just like Billy had done with the light of the moon, giving it the shape of a heart. This really got my attention and showed me he is still around us. The heart has become our favorite sign.

I still receive hearts to this day and they will always be my favorite sign. I am always in awe with every single one of them and say a thank you to Billy, with love.

It also goes to show if we focus too much on one type of sign, we mostly certainly miss others our loved ones send us. By focusing on the orbs and spirit energy in photos, I had missed seeing the spirit essence and heart signs until

Billy was finally able to get my attention. It goes to show how easily we can miss a sign by trying to focus on one or two types we are receiving and not seeing the other signs our loved ones are able to send us. Many are so subtle they can easily be missed.

At the same time, I was working on taking all of these photos, I also started working on the website in honor of Billy. I wanted to share my experience of what I had gone through, my feelings and heartbreak, and to making a connection with our son through a medium.

I spent six weeks getting our website together which was not an easy thing to do. It had been ten months since Billy had crossed over. Even after I had completed what I wanted to have on our website, I wasn't sure if it was any good or would be of any help to others. My web designer, Linda, told me the site was ready and to let her know when I would like it to go live. I was nervous and wasn't sure if I should redo the entire website or if what we had put together would work. The night I had to decide, I had a dream visit with Billy. The complete visit is in the chapter "My Signs."

As with all who grieve the loss of a loved ones, I still struggled a great deal. Just because I have been keeping busy with taking photos, our website, work, family, and more, grieving is still a big part of what I was dealing with at the time.

I kept doing the best I could working my day job as a mason contractor and still nearly every morning and evening going out to take a few photos. I would also take pictures inside, at weddings, family get–togethers, trips, and more. I continued to log pictures on my computer and on our website. I received many emails from people who had dealt with the loss of a loved one, as well. I spent a lot of time replying back to them. I also put together a picture book called *Signs from Our Loved Ones*, a collection of some of the spirit photos and images I have been able to take over the years. I also started to write articles on a number of grief/bereavement groups and memorial sites about my experiences.

In 2007, I was asked to do a radio interview. Doing this was something that never crossed my mind so I was *very* nervous. I agreed to do the show, but I don't recall the name of the program. It was hosted by Deborah Heneghan who also has a book called *Closer Than You Think*. Deborah was a great host which helped me deal with being so nervous. Over time, I have been on a number of radio shows including with Vicki Monroe, Bernard Ilsley, Christopher Reburn, and several interviews with Pamela Marie Edmunds.

Yes, I am still nervous every single time.

Through the years since Billy crossed over, I have collected around 80,000 spirit photos. I'm always in awe of every one I take. As time passes, my grieving lessens. However, it will never go away.

I have also been able to see some of these images with my eyes. While taking photos, as the flash goes off, I am able to see orbs around me. With the spirit essence images, what you see in the photo is only part of the entire image. However, I am able to see the spirit essences around me just inches away. It's so amazing. I am also able to see images by closing my eyes. I can also see much more, like people and mini movies, which is really cool.

Then, came Facebook.

At first, I really didn't do much on the social media site. I didn't think Facebook was for me, but I started my own page and soon starting searching for groups about grief/bereavement and groups about connecting with loved ones in heaven. I was then invited to a group called Visits from Heaven created by Josie Varga who I have come to be friends with as we both worked with the loss/crossing over of loved ones and the many signs they are able to send us. I read and shared postings and joined a number of other groups with people all on the same journey to help others with the loss crossing over a loved one and sign they are able to send us.

During this time, I started to create some of my own quotes which I added to a number of my photos. When I began sharing these on the group pages, it led me creating my own group, which I did in November 2011.

I named our group Signs from Our Loved Ones and invited Facebook people who had messaged me over the years to join. I had no idea how this would go or even if it would be anything people wanted to be a part of. I figured if we could have around five hundred members that came and went, that would be great. Boy, was I way off.

In about four and a half years (and as of the writing of this book), we have nearly 102,000 members on the Signs from Our Loved Ones group page and some 62,000 members on the Signs from Our Loved Ones – 2 group page. We hit five hundred members in a few months of starting the page and things took from there.

CHAPTER 3
Billy's Memorial Plaque

A few days after Billy crossed over, we made a roadside memorial garden at the scene of the accident, as many people do. We planted a number of plants and flowers to grow there in his memory. We also have a couple of posters with inspirational words, Billy's photo, and two plaques: one bought by my parents and another by some of Billy's friends. They both meant a great deal. I do have to say, I am sorry I never got to thank Billy's friends for making the plaque with the quote.

Maybe one day I will get to meet and thank them personally.

The plaque given by his friends was a 12" x 12" ceramic tile they leaned on a rock. We sprayed the tile with a clear sealer to help it hold up through all weather, but unfortunately, with time, it did not last. I took photos of it so I could remember word—for—word the entire quote and the peoples' names.

There was one last line at the bottom, but it wasn't clear enough for me to know what it said, but the rest of it went like this:

June 30, 1975 - June 26, 2004

Such a good friend

Taken so soon...

Always smiling, no matter what his mood...

Here for only a short time

But we knew him so well...

Though there is a hole that will never be

Filled, you'll be forever in our hearts...

We love you, Bill

Rest in peace

Tina, Jeannie, Victoria, Lisa

Thank you, Tina, Jeanie, Victoria, and Lisa. I was never able to thank you in person, but now I am able to do so here in my book, all be it twelve years later.

Thank you all so very much and with all of my heart. God Bless.

The property where Billy's roadside memorial garden was located was sold. We moved the entire tribute garden to our home and replanted everything in our backyard in a new memorial where everything still blooms and grows to this day.

Since I have a photo of the plaque given by Billy's friends, I plan to make a replica to add to the garden.

The plaque given by my parents was also transferred to our yard and reads:

If Tears Could Build A
Stairway, And Memories
A Lane, I'd Walk Right Up
To Heaven And Bring
You Home Again.

CHAPTER 4
Early Years of our Healing

The loss/crossing over of a loved one is the most devastating, heartbreaking, and painful event we will ever have to endure in our lifetime. Although we do go through many of the same emotions and feelings from the loss of a loved one, we all grieve differently, in our own way, and at our own pace.

However, it is the same for how we continue on our own journey as we slowly start to feel better. We will never "get over" the loss of a loved one. We simply do the best we can, one small step and one day at a time.

There are many ups and downs. Tears will fall many months after our loved one has crossed over and even years afterward. That's okay. It's a normal part of our grieving due to the love we have for the one we've lost.

With time, we are surround by more good days than bad and a knowledge that our loved one wants us to be happy and to live our lives to the fullest. This what brings their hearts great joy.

Here are some things you can do to get through and manage your grief:

- Draw closer to your friends, family, and loved ones. Spend more time with them, as well. Take the opportunity to spend all the time you can with them. These are the people who make a difference in our lives.

- Yes, you will need to take the time to grieve. Your daily routine will be disrupted. I was unable to work for six weeks following my son's death. I didn't care about paying bills, working, or anything. However, life does go on and you need to get back to your regular routine. When my wife and I both went back to work, we checked in with each other at noon every day by phone. Now, twelve years later, we still practice the same ritual because it's good to stay connected with your loved ones regularly.

- Create an online memorial page in honor of your loved one, just as we did for our son. Many sites are free and/or come with a small fee. This is a wonderful way to keep photos, comments, stories, and more to help keep the memory of your loved one close. Some examples are:

  ✓ Virtual Memorial

  ✓ WebHealing.com

✓ MemoryOf.com

✓ Legacy.com

- Create memorial apparel in honor of your loved one. We have a page on www.zazzle.com celebrating Billy through memorabilia. This website is a place to create many different items for all occasions, including (but not limited to) refrigerator magnets, bracelets, photo designs, T-shirts, Christmas ornaments and so many more ideas.

- Make a website or blog. A website costs money, but it's also a way to share your story and to help others who might be going through the same thing. There are some free places to start a website, but there can be limits. You'll want to do your research. One place, www.wordpress.com, is wonderful to create a blog to share your own experience about your loved one. It is also very easy to use. I have a blog through WordPress called Signs From Our Loved Ones. Our memorial sites to Billy are: www.signsfromourlovedones.com and www.oursonbilly.com.

- Collect some of the signs your loved one uses to get your attention, like coins, feathers, heart-shaped objects, rocks, etc.

- Build a memorial garden for your loved ones who have crossed over. You can create the look you want with countless different plants, flowers, a fountain, figurines, and statues, if you have space. Even if you do not have the room or live in an apartment, you can always create a small-scale planter which will work just in the same way and you'll be able to enjoy it year round. You can even add symbols of the signs you receive from your loved ones like pennies, feathers, or however they contact you. Not only do we collect these signs, but we have incorporated a few of them into our home and garden, such as a penny I found with our son's birth year. I bought a heart-shaped wedding cake pan about six inches tall which I added high strength concrete and a red dye. When the concrete started to cure, I added the penny in the center and it is now part of our memorial garden. The list is endless of what you are all able to create in honor of you loved one. As always, only do what you feel comfortable with and do it at your own pace.

- Every year, my wife and I add a photo and a few words on Billy's birthday and Christmas time in our local newspaper. You can certainly do the same.

- At family weddings, set a small table and have photos of your loved ones who have crossed over. That way, all family members can see the memorial and know the people who helped make their family special. It also brings them closer to the special event.

- Keep your loved one "alive" by sharing stories about him or her. Through our story—telling, Billy is still very much in our lives and always will be a part of our family. Again, do only what you are comfortable with and know some may feel uncomfortable sharing. However, in time, they may open up and join in the great comfort and joy.

- I have been moved to write inspiring and helpful quotes, many of them on photo signs from our son. These quotes help bring comfort and healing to my family and others.

- My wife, Jo—Anne, collects Christmas ornaments in honor of our son and hangs them on the Christmas tree every year. You, too, can do this by purchasing special ornaments or making them yourself.

- Every Tuesday, we have dinner and a movie night with some family. Having a regular family event like this keeps us grounded and immersed in the lives of those we love. You can plan a game night, dinner, movie... anything.

- I have done several radio shows talking about the loss/crossing over of Billy, my experiences, and the many signs Billy has given us over the years to let us know our loved ones are truly still so very much around us with all of their love. You can look at ways you can share you experiences and stories that might help others going through the same thing.

- Create a Facebook group or page to draw in people with similar experiences. Our first group is called Signs From Our Loved Ones and is open to the public. The second Facebook page is a closed group called Signs From Our Loved Ones—2. The closed group is for those who wish to keep their postings private so only other group members can read them. Our groups are for those who have dealt with the loss/crossing over of a loved to read and share about their loss, grief, heartbreak, pain, recovery, comfort, healing, guidance, support, compassion, and to share the many different ways our loved ones are able to connect with us, letting us know they are still by our side. Our two groups are a positive place to help and learn from one another that we are not alone in what we are going through.

These are just some of the things we have done and continue to work on every day. Most of all, we are always there for one another. There are countless different ways you can develop and create your own projects in honor of your loved one.

Simply follow your heart.

CHAPTER 5
Grieving and Guilt

Grieving

Grieving the loss/crossing over of a loved one is different for everyone, we all grieve differently and in our own way and timeframe. In truth, we will grieve until the day we are reunited with our loved ones; the day we cross over ourselves. We learn with time to do the best we can which is one small step and one day at a time. The pain lessens, but it doesn't complete go away.

We grieve because we love. Our loved ones who have crossed over are still so very much around us, by our side to help and guide us with only unconditional love for us. We do whatever will help us to keep going. The loss/crossing over of a loved one is the most devastating and unfathomable pain we will ever have to experience and endure.

It will bring out many different emotions such as anger, shock, denial, numbness, sadness, guilt, anxiety, fear, depression, loneliness, isolation, confusion, overwhelmed, loss or gain of weight, lack of sleep, just to name a few.

Is it possible to recover and to start living your life again and to be happy? Absolutely. Know that your loved ones are watching over you and doing all they can to help you along the way. When they see us begin our healing and start to live our lives again, it brings joy to their heart.

It will be an up and down journey, but with time things will get better, all in our own timeframe. You will be a different you; how much so is up to you. Our loved ones want us to be happy and to live our lives to the fullest.

There are no magic pills you can take and wake up the next morning thinking all will be okay. It doesn't work that way. Grieving is a slow process with many different emotions we all go through and all a very normal part of our grieving process and that's okay. We have to do our part and our loved ones who have crossed over will do everything they can to help us with all of their love.

Always remember, the separation from our loved ones is only temporary. We will be reunited with our loved ones the day our own journey has been completed with the greatest of joy and love. In the meantime, they are by our side with all of their love to help and guide us. Just listen to the whispers of your heart.

We are not alone with all that we are going through with the loss/crossing over of a loved one. We all mostly go through the same thing, just at times in a different way and timeframe and that is okay. Some of the stages of grief are:

- Shock and Denial — disbelief that this could even be happening,

- Extreme feelings of pain and heartbreak — what at times seem unbearable to handle.

- Anger — at the world, God, people around you, those who may be involved, even at your loved one for crossing over, even mad at yourself.

- Guilt — for not being able to have prevented your loved ones from crossing over.

- Bargaining — with God to bring back your loved one, to take you instead, and/or being able to have done something to have your loved one here again.

- Depression — not wanting to do anything or go anywhere, losing weight, no laughter or smiles, not caring about anything.

- Loneliness — feeling of now being left alone since your loved one has crossed over

- Feeling overwhelmed – no longer having your loved one around to help you and dealing with all that you are now going through.

These are some of the emotions we go through during our stages of grieving. It's completely normal. We may all react differently and some of the steps of grief may affect people in various ways. That is also normal.

Just know our loved ones who have crossed over are still so very much by our side with the greatest of love to help and guide us through all of this. They know exactly what we are going through, what we are feeling, what we are thinking about, how much we miss them, and the love we have for them.

Our loved ones will always be by our side to help us along our own journey; they know we need the time to grieve. To our loved ones, seeing us slowly become happy again, living our lives to the fullest brings them great joy on the other side. Our loved ones know we have our own journey to follow and they know with all of their heart we will never forget them.

After the loss/crossing over of Billy, I was not doing very well and was asked this same question on two occasions, months apart. The first time was about eight months after our son crossed over. My grief was so deep that the question didn't sink in at the time, but it stuck into the back of my mind. The second time I was asked the exact same question it *did* sink in. It went like this...

I was asked: What if I had crossed over and Billy was grieving for me the way I was for him? How would that make me feel in heaven?

What a great question.

I answered by saying I would be very sad to see him grieving for me as deeply as I am for him. From heaven, in my spirit form, I would do everything I could to help my son start to heal. I would let him know I am still around him and by his side with the greatest of love.

I would let him know I am okay, safe, happy, and filled with only unconditional love. I would try to find a way to let Billy know our separation is only temporary and that one day we will be reunited again once his own journey has been completed.

Most of all, I would let Billy know I am still and will always be by his side to help and guide him along his own journey and that I love him with all of my heart, always and forever.

You can bet our loved one who has crossed over is doing the exact same thing for us.

I remember all too well my early stages of my grieving. The pain felt so great at times it was overwhelming and I felt I could not possibly survive another second, but I did…

Or another minute, but I did…

Or another hour, but I did…

Or another day, but I did…

You will, too.

Guilt

The more we share the more we can help one another to know we are not alone with all we are going through from the loss/crossing over of a loved one. Guilt may come in different forms. Maybe it was our relationship or something we may have done or said. Maybe if we had gone with them, stopped them from going, made a phone call, or even feel badly for smiling again, laughing, being happy, enjoying life, or countless other reasons… we may feel guilty.

This was the case for me thinking I could have done something to prevent the accident which took the life of our son. The night Billy had his accident, I had a vivid dream where I knew someone in my family had died. I could see people gathered at the funeral, but I could not see Billy. I awoke nearly in tears and almost roused my wife, thinking we should call our two sons to make sure they were both okay. After a minute or two, I decide not to bother her and thought it was simply a nightmare. With some tossing and turning, I went back to sleep.

The next morning, the dream was still on my mind as many of our family went out to breakfast to say good-bye to my sister, as I've already shared. When my sister, June, gave us the news that one of our cousins was killed while riding his ATV, I was shocked to receive confirmation at 10 a.m. that it was actually Billy who had died.

I carried the feelings of guilt for some time thinking if I had only made a phone call, Billy might still be with us. However, "what iffing" doesn't do us any good, it only holds us back. I was able to let go of those guilty feelings eight months later during the reading with the medium, who relayed a message from Billy who told us there was nothing on earth that could have changed the event. Billy told us it was his time, his journey, and what he was here to accomplish was completed. It was time for him to cross over and for me to please let go of any feeling of guilt.

Our loved ones do not want us to have these feelings of guilt for one second longer. All they have for us is unconditional love. We are all here to learn, experience, grow, and, most of all, to love. The feelings of guilt will only hold us back, we don't need to hold on to any feelings of guilt. Let it go.

CHAPTER 6
Ways to Honor and Signs to See

Ways to Honor

We have received many emails, messages, and postings on our Facebook group page asking what are some of the ways a person can honor a loved one. Well, it's whatever way you feel comfortable doing something in their honor.

Here are a few things we have also done in honor of Billy:

- Have a photo of them on your wall/desk with a poem to bring you some comfort.

- Make a memorial blanket or quilt from some of their clothing for a keepsake.

- There are a number of websites that will also help you make a memorial/tribute video in honor of your loved ones.

- Release balloons on their birthday or angel–versary

- Write a poem in their honor

- Keep a journal like you are talking to your loved one. They do hear every single word we say, so write about them.

- On their birthday, have their favorite meal, play their favorite music, or watch their favorite movie.

These are just a few samples of some of the many ways you can honor a loved one who has crossed over and remember they are and always will be around you with the greatest of love, by your side to help and guide you.

Signs to See

Our loved one is able to send us a sign or message in countless ways to get our attention and let us know they are still around us in the form of spirit/energy. They are more alive than they ever were here in the physical world. Our loved one knows when we are thinking about them in our minds or out loud. They hear every single word we say to them. They know what is in our hearts, how much we miss them, and of all the love we have for them.

Our loved one uses many different ways to connect with us, like a familiar scent/smell, a song, numbers, something they loved like birds, coins, cigars, orbs/spirit energy, perfume, butterflies, dragonflies, ladybugs, collectibles such as angel figurines, hearts, etc. The list is endless.

The best way to look at a sign—if you feel what you see/receive is a sign to/for you—is to simply follow your heart. That is all that really matters.

- Coins – pennies, nickels, dimes, quarters, you name it. A loved one is able to use them to let us know they are right there with us. Look at the date as it may be something significant or meaningful like the year they were born, married, and so forth.

- Butterflies, dragonflies, and ladybugs – these insects can be influenced by our loved one to get our attention. Our loved ones will often have the insect fly around and land on us, especially when we are thinking about them or feeling down.

- Scent/smell – is another way our loved one is able to get our attention to by connecting their memory to a specific smell like perfume, cigars, food, flowers, aftershave, etc.

- Music/song –our loved one can connect with us when we hear a special song you both loved, a song with special meaning, one which brings great memories or brings them to mind when you hear the music and/or lyrics.

- Feathers – it does not matter what type of feather a loved one uses to get it touch with us. The important thing is they have been able to get your attention and let you know they are still very much around you.

- Numbers – number combinations can be in the form of a loved one's age, date of birth, favorite number, their sports uniform number, the time they were born or crossed over and much more. Pay attention to seeing the same numbers repeated on a clock, license plate, signs, coins, clothing, or anywhere.

- Birds/animals –our loved one might send you a sign in the form of their favorite type of bird like a red cardinal, songbird, eagle, dove, and others. They might land close by, fly around you, sit on a fence and watch, or sing out to you.

- Collectibles – if your love one collected anything particular, they might reach out to you through that particular symbol, such as a collection of angels figurines, photos, jewelry, clothing, knick–knacks, sports memorabilia, etc.

- Hearts — can come to you as a sign in many ways: on a neckless, jewelry, heart—shaped clouds, heart—shaped sign, on a book cover, a logo, heart—shaped piece of paper, heart—shaped lights, license plate, clothing, an ornament, greeting card… the list goes on.

It does not matter how many signs I am able to receive from Billy. I am in awe of every single one of them, knowing he is still trying to reach out to me from the other side.

CHAPTER 7
Frequently Asked Questions

Why are we here?

We come here in the physical world to grow, to learn lessons, to teach, to experience life, the joy and the heartbreaks, to accomplish things, to work and learn from one another, to learn how to live with one another, to live life to the fullest, and to grow spiritually, and the greatest of all, to love. All of these revolve around the most important thing of all... love, to become a better us. In some way, no matter if a loved one's lifetime is only for a few minutes, days, weeks, months, a few years, or a very long lifetime, there is always a reason, lessons, experiences, spiritual growth, and love to the meaning of their time, however, short or long it may be. It is much faster to learn these lessons in the physical world because we feel the pain, heartbreak, joy, happiness, love, and everything else we go through in our physical form. In our true form—our soul—our spirit energy consists of unconditional love and has no negative feeling, no hate, no anger, no grudges, nor any ill will towards anyone.

Do our loved ones who have crossed over know how much we miss and loved them?

Yes, they absolutely know how much we miss them and how much love we have for them. They have only changed back into their true form of spirit/energy. They are able to feel our love and that we miss them.

If we move to a new home or country, do our loved ones follow us or do they lose where we go?

Our loved one, in their true form of spirit/energy, know exactly where we are at all times and we are never left alone. They are wherever we go or move. Our loved ones will never lose track of us, no matter where we are.

Do our loved ones who have crossed over ever get angry with us?

Impossible. Our loved ones have unconditional love for us. They never get angry with us in any way and there's never anything negative. When they cross over it is all about love.

Can our loved ones hear us when we talk to them?

Absolutely, they can hear every word we say to them out loud or in our minds. Our loved ones hear every single word we say or think about them, always. Feel free to talk to your loved ones at any time.

When our loved ones cross over, are they really okay?

Yes, our loved ones are fine, actually they are perfect. They are back in their true and our true form of spirit/energy and are no longer in any pain. They're not sad or negative about anything and all they have is unconditional love, safe, happy and still by our side.

Are our loved ones with us during the holidays and other family events?

Yes, our loved ones are always around us, watching over us and all that we do and experience here in the physical world. They are always by our side with the greatest of love.

Can our loved ones see us?

Yes, they can see us and are by our side seeing what we are going through and following us during our own journey. They see all the things all of us accomplishing, learning, growing, wedding, birthdays, holidays, our loved one see all we do during our lifetime. They are right there with us, always.

Can our loved ones guide us during our own journey?

Yes, our loved ones are always around us to help and guide us along in our own journey. We can always ask them for help and guidance. Our loved ones, spirit guides, angels, and more are always around us for guidance, but it's our choice/free will to decide our own course of action. Just listen to the whispers of your heart.

Do our loved ones want us to feel guilty because they have crossed over or for issues which may have occurred during our lifetime together?

No, our loved ones do not hold on to any feelings of guilt and neither should we because it only holds us back. All they want is for us to be happy, to live our lives to the fullest, and to do the best that we can.

Do our loved ones want us to stay in deep grief for them?

No, our loved ones know what we are going through, how much we miss them, and of all the love we have for them. They know we need to grieve for them and that it is different for everyone. In reality, we grieve for them the rest of our lives. We need time to learn to continue to live our lives. The separation from our loved ones is only temporary. We will be reunited the day our own journey has been completed. In fact, our loved ones know it takes time and they want so much for us to live our lives to the fullest, to be happy, experience all we can, and to love with all of our heart. This will bring our loved ones in heaven the greatest of joy.

When we cross over, will we recognize our loved ones who have crossed over to heaven before us?

Instantly. We will recognize each other right away and many other loved ones who have crossed over before.

Does the bond of love between us and our loved ones continue when they cross over?

Yes, love is the bond that can never be broken. When our loved ones cross over to heaven, they carry with them all of the love with them. It is for always and forever. Love it everything.

Can our loved one send us signs in many different ways?

Yes, our loved ones are able to connect with us in countless ways to get our attention. Some signs are subtle and can easily be missed, like a feather or coin in your path, a song, a scent, etc. Other signs are more obvious like a dream visit connecting with your loved one in great detail, seeing symbolic signs of hearts or certain numbers, letters, butterflies/dragonflies landing or around you or even seeing your loved one right in front of you. Always remember, all signs are special, meaningful, important, comforting, profound, and sent to us with unconditional love to let us know they are still very much around us with all of their love.

Can our loved ones visit us in a dream visit?

Absolutely. Dream visits are a wonderful way to be able to connect, see, talk with, get messages, and to receive some comfort and a peace of mind from a loved one. When our loved ones visit us in a dream visit, it is always done with unconditional love, never to scare us and never anything negative or hurtful toward us; only with unconditional love.

Why do we grieve so deeply?

We grieve so deeply because we love so deeply. That is the price for loving someone, which we would never change.

What is "crossing over?"

Crossing over is a term for going to heaven, the other side, the hereafter, and the afterlife—all the same places, just a different names. When our physical body dies, our soul/spirit crosses over to a new plane of existence and we are greeted by many loved ones with the greatest of joy and love.

What is an orb?

Orbs, better known as spirit energy, are one of the ways our loved ones, spirit guides, angels, etc., are able to use their energy to show us they're around us. Orbs may show up as balls of light in photos, videos, or can even be seen by the naked eye. It's like our loved ones are poking through the thin veil which separates the physical world from the spiritual world. They are called orbs because they are round. It is also one of the least amount of energy they are able to use to get our attention they are still very much around us with all of their love, at times even being able to see images in the orb/spirit energy. No matter what color you see orbs/spirit energy, they are always of love.

Can I ask my loved one for a specific sign?

You may certainly ask your loved one who has passed for a certain sign, depending on what means something or is significant to you or the two of you, like their favorite number, familiar smell/scent, maybe they love butterflies, a specific song, birds, dream visit, coins, the list is endless. If you don't receive your sign immediately, don't be discouraged. Just keep your eyes and ears open and keep an open heart, the signs will come.

How do I know if what I see, feel, smell is really a sign?

The best way to interpret whether something is a sign is if you feel it in your heart. Just follow what your heart is telling you. At times, look for signs which repeat themselves often in your daily life. Keep a notebook of the signs you see and what they mean to you as you continue to recognize them in the future.

Do our loved ones feel hurt if we are not by their side when they die/crossover?

No, their feelings are not hurt in any way. All they have is love. To them, the second they cross over, they are still very much around us. Trivial matters no longer matter. It's all about the love.

Why do people use the term "loss of a loved one" when someone crosses over to heaven?

Many use the term "loss of a loved one" and some prefer to use just crossed over, transcended to heaven, gone to heaven, or something else. In the end, it doesn't matter. You'll be told by well–meaning friends and acquaintances, "I'm sorry to hear about the loss of your loved one," as meaning only the physical "loss" of a loved one. Of course, we miss their physical presence, being able to see them, hear their voice, feel their touch, smell their scent, and just being around them enjoying their company. It is okay to feel the loss of their physical presence because we love so deeply. In reality, we never really "lose" a loved one, because their soul/spirit energy can never die.

Will my significant loved one be upset if I find a new love to spend the rest of my life with?

No, they will not be upset in any way because all they have for us is unconditional love. They want us to be happy and to live our lives to the fullest. If meeting and falling in love with someone makes us happy, that will bring our loved one great joy to see.

Is it normal to have a breakdown into tears even years after loved one has crossed over to heaven?

Of course, it is. It's all a normal part of our grieving process. We mourn deeply because we love so deeply.

Where is heaven, the hereafter, the afterlife, the other side, etc.?

Heaven is all around us. We are not able to see heaven, although a few have seen a glimpse. Heaven, or the spiritual world, vibrates at a higher frequency than we are able to see, which also means our loved ones, spirit guides, angels, and more all of unconditional love, are only a thin veil away from us here in the physical world. The message relayed to us from our son, Billy, was put this way: Think of the most beautiful, happiest, fulfilling, joyful, exciting, and loved day. Now, multiply that by an infinite number and that is how much better heaven is…

no doubt. It's all around us; it vibrates on a higher level than we are able to see and is not some faraway place in the sky.

Why can't I see my loved ones like some people can?

Our grief, heartbreak, emotions, guilt, beliefs, fears, and more all have a part in what we are able to handle. We are all capable of seeing our loved ones, and the countless signs they send us, also bitterness, negativity, and how in most part, how the world wants us to believe, has influenced us. The more open we are, the more we will be able to understand and see. Young children seem to be able to see and talk to loved ones who have crossed over and even give us wonderful signs and message that loved ones are still very much around us, they have not yet been influenced or jaded by society. The more everyone begins to share their experiences and not be influenced by how others want us to believe, the more others will start to share their own experiences. The more open we are the more we will understand and see. Keep an open heart.

How can our loved ones who have crossed over be with loved ones here in the physical world in different places at the same time?

When a loved one crosses over, they return to our true

form, spirit/energy and can be any place at any time and many places all at the same time. We have to remember when we return to our true form, our spirit/energy, we are able to be everywhere because we are no longer bound by the physical world. We are free to be everywhere and not tied down by a physical body.

Can a reading by a medium help in my healing process?

Yes, absolutely. A reading by a medium can be a great help in our healing process as it did for me. It was the start of my path to healing. There is no magic pill that will make everything fine the next day. Nothing works that way. However, having a reading and possibly receiving messages from your loved ones can help you on your way to healing from your pain, to help bring some comfort, peace of mind, and peace to your heart.

Do our loved ones always put the sign in front of us themselves to get our attention?

No, not always, but they can put a thought in our mind to influence us to look in a certain area to see something (a sign) they want us to see to get our attention.

Is there ever any reason to be scared or afraid?

No. Our connection with a loved one on the other side is all about love. It's the physical world that has created all of the negative stuff which now exist in our minds.

What is a repetitive sign?

A repetitive sign is receiving the same sign over and over again, whether butterflies, cardinals, a song, coin, numbers, word/words, smell/scent, and countless more. A way for our loved ones to let us know they are trying to get our attention they are still so very much by our side with all of their love.

Do our loved ones miss us?

Yes, absolutely they do but in a different way. We have to remember now that our loved ones have crossed over they are back in their one true form—spirit/energy—and are; therefore, still so very much around us and closer to us than they ever were here in the physical world. They know what we are going through, how we are feeling, and what is in our hearts.

Do those who commit suicide, do they cross over to heaven?

Yes. It does not matter how a loved one's physical life ends, they all cross over to heaven, greeted by many loved ones with the greatest of joy and love. They are still so very much around us with all of their love. They all know how much we miss them and of all the love we have for them. All they have for us is unconditional love.

Do our pets cross over? If so, will they recognize us when we cross over?

I believe our pets, along with all animals, cross over to heaven and our pets will greet us along with all of our loved ones with the greatest of joy and love.

A question I get asked often is: How do you know this?

The easiest way to answer this question is I've learned from my own experiences after the loss/crossing over of our son Billy, on June 26, 2004. From receiving signs to catching orb photos to my dreams, books, programs, websites, our group page, talking with others and visiting with a few mediums. All the messages add up to a conclusion that Billy is still with me which bring me comfort and great joy. Through the formulation of our online community, I have been able to read experiences from so many people from all over the world who all acknowledge the same things I've been through. It's comforting talking to people, hearing what they've been through, and knowing we're not alone. I'm always learning from others and I hope they can learn from me, as well. In the end, follow what your heart is telling you.

CHAPTER 8
My Experience with Signs

When I received the first sign from Billy, I didn't realize was a sign at all. It wasn't until a month or so since Billy had crossed over. My wife and I had fallen asleep and in the middle of the night, we were awakened by our doorbell ringing. I quickly got up, put on my pants, and hurried to the door to see who could possibly be disturbing us so late at night. I looked through the window and could not see anyone. I then opened the door, walked out on the porch, glanced around, and still saw no one. Even though there was a light rain falling, I walked out into the driveway barefooted with only a pair of jeans on. We live in the countryside with no sidewalks, so there really wasn't a place for anyone to be walking around on the street.

After a while, I decide to get back into the house since I was getting wet. As I hustled back up to the porch, I noticed there were no wet footprints which would have been made by whoever rang the doorbell. My own wet footprints appeared when I moved around the porch. Since I was tired, I went inside the house and back to bed, not concerning myself with the footprints. I told my wife no one had been at the door and didn't know what had happened. In the passing weeks, we decided the whole thing may have been a sign, but we weren't sure. All I had to do was to follow my heart and it would have let me know right away this was Billy's way of letting us know he is still around us. It wasn't until eight months after he crossed over when we had our reading with Vicki Monroe. She told us it was Billy who rang the doorbell along with my mom's dad to let us know he is around us.

Dream visit – My first dream visit with Billy came about ten months after he had crossed over. At the time, I had been working on putting together a website about our story (www.oursonbilly.com). I had been working on the site for about six weeks. My web designer had me look it over when she was finished to see if I was okay with everything. When it was about to go live on the internet, I was so nervous, I kept going over the website to make sure everything was the way I wanted it to be presented, but not sure if what I had worked on would be any good to be of any help to anyone. I had to let her know one way or another if I thought our website was ready or if she needed to do more work. I went to sleep thinking about what to do and during the night, I had this dream visit with Billy.

The dream was so vivid and colorful. I was sitting at a large desk with nothing on it. I looked up and saw Billy walking into the room with the huge smile on his face and a piece of paper in his hand. I watched him come right up to me. I was so happy to see him. Billy didn't say a word and handed me this piece of paper. I glanced at the paper and all it had on it was a huge "A." Billy smiled at me and walked out of the room. I wasn't sure what the "A" on the paper meant until I woke up the next morning and told my wife about the dream visit. She reminded me of how I'd been thinking about the website and not sure if it would be of any help to others. Jo– Anne told me it was Billy's way of letting me know the website is good to go live on the internet.

I was so happy to have the dream visit and to see Billy again. I did not even think about the dream being a message about the website. I gave the web designer the go–ahead and everything worked out well. When we had another reading with Vicki Monroe a few months later, she confirmed another message from Billy that the website was ready.

We never know when, how, where a message from a loved one will come our way. We need to keep an open mind and, even better, an open heart.

Another way Billy has been able to get my attention is with the motion sensor lights we have on our garage.

One day, while I was sitting in our backyard thinking about Billy, I noticed the motion light kept blink on and off for no reason. There was no one around to make the light blink, no wind of any kind to make any tree branch to trigger the light or anything. I couldn't help but wonder if Billy was making the light blink this way to get my attention, so I decide to try something. I walked up closer to the light and decide to ask a few questions. I asked Billy if it was him to please let me know by blinking the light two times for "yes." I waited and the light blinked twice. I repeated the same question and again the light blinked two times. I asked more questions this way and Billy would answer. It was so amazing.

It was the same with the night light I have in my office. At times, I would be working on my computer staring at the screen, and the night light would start blinking on and off. I would notice Billy would move the cursor in different directions on my screen which would get my attention and put a smile on my face knowing he was right by my side.

My wife called me to dinner one night while I was in my office. When I got up to leave, I could clearly see Billy sitting on the couch with a big smile on his face. He didn't say a word and looked exactly as he did before he crossed over. The moment only lasted a brief few seconds, but it was so comforting to actually see him and know he was happy. This helped bring me some great comfort I needed at the time, a peace of mind and great joy to experience.

Another dream visit featured a few of us all gathered in what appeared to be an old time general store. We were hanging around telling stories. I do not remember what they were, but we are having a great time. Billy told us a joke that was so funny (again I do not remember, I wish I could) and we all started to laugh very hard, so much that I could see everyone's faces turning red. I was laughing so hard that I started to wake up. I did not want to wake up my wife, so I had to bury my face into my pillow to muffle the sound. It took some time, but I was finally able to stop laughing and go back to sleep. I was hoping to return to the dream with Billy and everyone else, but it never happened.

I am so very thankful for the wonderful fun dream visit; one I needed at the time. While doing research on the many different ways our loved ones are able to connect with us, I found that our loved ones are able to let us know they are very much around us, as well as our spirit guides, angels, ascended masters, pets/animals, and more all with love. They are able to use their energy to show up in photos, videos, and even seeing them with your eyes to get our attention they are all around us. It is also one of the least amount of energy they can use for us to see them in photos or with our own eyes. I thought to myself I can take pictures so I decided this was one of the ways I would try to connect with Billy. This started about ten months or so after he crossed over. On my first time I tried taking photos, it worked. I was so excited I was able to purposely take spirit photos.

To see some of the amazing spirit photos, visit our website www.oursonbilly.com.

You do not need any expensive camera or equipment of any kind. I mostly use a couple of cameras at the same time. All you really need is an open mind, an open heart, and, of course, a camera. I still use the Kodak Easy–Share 3.2 megapixel camera, a Kodak Easy–Share 6.1 megapixel camera Z760, and a Nikon Coolpix 12 megapixel camera. I will also use the inexpensive $4 disposable cameras. I love using the digital camera the most because I can download them right away and see what images I captured. I have tens of thousands of amazing spirit energy photos and they are always of unconditional love.

After I finished taking photos for the day, I always say thank you for showing up and giving me these signs.

To continue with the "orbs" spirit energy as a sign, I am able to see them while taking photos by holding my camera about eight to ten inches away. When the flash goes off, I can see the orbs all around me; only inches away. Many times, what you see in the photos are merely a small part of what I am able to see with my naked eye. They are small, but very bright lights. They will move in many directions or will draw shapes, like hearts.

Feathers – Two of my favorite signs with feathers:

> 1. One day, as I was getting into my truck for work, I saw a beautiful feather only inches from my door handle. It was Billy's way of letting me know he was with me.

> 2. My sister and parents have a cockatoo. While visiting one time, my mom came up to me and gave me a lovely red feather. She told me it was important for me to have it and it was meant for me. I still have the feather. Our loved ones not only send us signs for us to see, but also ones can be given to us by family, friends, and strangers. We never know what form, how, when, where, or from whom a sign will come our way.

Hearts – are one of my favorite if not my favorite signs other than actually seeing Billy. As I've stated, I had been receiving signs from Billy in different forms—love them all—but on October 21, 2005, I had to take a double take with one photo. It looked like the moon was in the shape of a perfect heart. I zoomed in and sure enough it was. I was in such awe and could not believe our loved ones could possibly send us a sign like this. I started looking back and found more and have since received many more heart−shaped images of the moon, street lights, Christmas tree lights, and in the months and years following, I have received signs in the form of heart−shaped clouds, heart− shaped rocks, water images in the shape of hearts, and many other heart−shaped images of all types from our son letting us know he will always be with us.

Coins − are another way my wife and I receive signs from our son, Billy. For me, it's been pennies, of which one of them had the year of his birthday.

When it comes to a sign, if you feel in your heart they are a sign to you, then it is and just follow your heart. That is all that really matters and if you are wondering who the sign may be from, go with who comes to mind first.

CHAPTER 9
Inspirational Quotes

The following are some of the quotes I've shared on my Facebook group pages:

If our loved ones who have crossed over could send us all a short message, it would go something like this.

I am okay

I am always with you

I will never leave you

Never feel guilty about living your life

I know what you are going through, how much you miss me and of all the love you have for me.

I hear every word you say to me, aloud or in your mind.

I see you,

You are never alone

I am by your side to help and guide you with the greatest of love for you

Be happy, it brings me great joy

Most of all − I love you

All I have for you is unconditional love

~ ~ ~ ~ ~

Always remember that our separation from our loved ones who have crossed over is only temporary.
When our own
Journey has been completed, we to will cross over and be Reunited with our loved ones, with the greatest of joy and Love.

~ ~ ~ ~ ~

Our Loved Ones
Are only
A tear away
A smile away
A breath away
A dream away
A thought away
A heartbeat away
A very thin veil away
A heavenly sign away
Our loved ones are always around us, with only
The greatest of love for us... unconditional love.

~ ~ ~ ~ ~

Grieving

There is no wrong or right way to
Grieve the loss/crossing over of a
Loved one.
It's done your way at your
Own pace and timeframe.
It's different for everyone, we all
Grieve in our own way.
You take the time you need,
It's one very small step and one
Day at a time.
Know that our loved ones who have
Crossed over are by our side to help
Guide us.
We never "get over it" never happen
We learn to adjust our lives and do the
Best that we can, our own way.
Always remember the separation from
our loved ones is
Only temporary, we will be reunited

~ ~ ~ ~ ~

You will never have to worry that your
Loved one who has crossed over is ever
Angry, won't forgive you or has anything

Negative towards you... never happen
All they have is unconditional love for us.

~ ~ ~ ~ ~

The Bond Of Love

Between us and our loved ones
And our loved ones who have crossed
Over to heaven, can never be broke.
The bond of love is for always and forever.

~ ~ ~ ~ ~

When our loved ones cross over.
They take back with them, their memories the
Best part of themselves and most of all their love

~ ~ ~ ~ ~

Signs From Our Loved Ones

All signs from our loved ones are comforting
All signs are very special
All signs are very important
All signs are very meaningful
All signs are absolutely profound
It does not matter what type of sign you receive

From your loved one… they are all so very special
Always done with the greatest of love… unconditional
love.

~ ~ ~ ~ ~

Even though our loved ones are no longer here with us
In their physical form, they are still so very much around
us.
It's only their physical body that ceases to exist, the real us
Is spirit/energy, which cannot die and is very much alive
and well
With memories, personality and most of all their love.

~ ~ ~ ~ ~

The greatest way to connect with our loved
Who have crossed over is to listen to the
Whispers of you heart.

~ ~ ~ ~ ~

I will always keep your memory alive
I will always talk about you
I will always keep you in my heart
I will always take things one day at a time

I will always live my life at my own pace, living again
I will always miss you
I will always love you
I will be seeing you again
Until we meet again.

~ ~ ~ ~ ~

Don't worry about tomorrow
today is difficult enough, just
get through today. One moment,
to one minute, to one hour, to one
day… this day.
One very small step and one day
at a time.
Whenever possible to be there for
one another to help bring some
comfort and peace of mind.

~ ~ ~ ~ ~

Memories
When our loved ones crossover
not only do they take all of their
love for us when they crossover,
but also take all of their memories with them.

Every Step of the Way

Know that even if we are not
able to see, hear or feel our
loved ones around us...
They are and always will be by
our side to help and guide us
along our own journey.
Our loved ones know we have
our own path to follow, and they
will be there for us, every step of
the way and with all of their love.

~ ~ ~ ~ ~

Tears

Suffering the loss/crossing over
of a loved one will cause us to
shed countless tears to flow and
it helps us in our healing and that's okay.
Tears will flow, days, week's months
and years later and that's okay.
Tears may come what seems out of
nowhere and even many years later
and that's okay.
Tears are all a part of our love and
healing and that's okay.

~ ~ ~ ~ ~

Talking To Our Loved Ones

When we talk to our loved ones.
they hear every single word we say
or think about them, every word.
Always remember, our loved ones,
their spirit energy is always around us.
We may not feel or see them around us
but their energy/soul/spirit, is always
with us as is all of their love.
Love is everything.

~ ~ ~ ~ ~

Take Time for Yourself

Our loved ones know we also need
to take time for ourselves, time to
relax have fun and enjoy the day,
is okay and to never ever feel guilty
for doing so.
When our loved ones see us taking
some time to ourselves, it brings them
great joy to see, they know this also helps
us with our healing.
Always one small step and one day at a time.

~ ~ ~ ~ ~

Hugs

We don't always need to have
to say much of anything, at
times all that is needed is a
Hug.
It's something all have to
offer and to share with those
who are grieving.
A simple hug can be a great
comfort to those who are
dealing with the loss/crossing
over of a loved one.

~ ~ ~ ~ ~

Love

It is all about the
love
It has always been
about the
Love
it will always be
About the Love

~ ~ ~ ~ ~

Love Is Everything

The only thing that is
real is the Love
In the end all that really
matters is the Love.

~ ~ ~ ~ ~

Holding Someone's Hand

Sometimes just taking someone's
hand and holding it, is a very welcoming
comfort to someone who is grieving and so very needed.
It may not seem like much to us at the
time, but to those who are grieving, it
can mean a great deal to them.

~ ~ ~ ~ ~

Always Around Us

You may not see us, hear us or feel us around you
But we are absolutely very much with you and send
you signs in countless different ways to get your attention
we are still very much by your side with all of our love.
Our bond of love can never be broken, always and
forever.

~ ~ ~ ~ ~

Loving Us

Our loved ones who have crossed over
will never ever forget about us... impossible.
They can never ever stop loving us... impossible.
Our loved ones are still and always around us
with all of their love.

~ ~ ~ ~ ~

Never alone

No matter where you are, you are never
left alone, we have many loved ones,
spirit guides, angels and more all of
unconditional love always with us......always

~ ~ ~ ~ ~

I Love You

A message which all of our loved ones
want with all of their hearts for us to know.

~ ~ ~ ~ ~

From Our Loved Ones

With every breath you take,

With every step you take,

We are there.

With every tear you have,

With every smile you have,

We are there.

With every thought you have,

With every feeling you have,

We are there.

With every lesson you have,

With every experience you have,

We are there.

With every heartbreak you have,

With every joy you have,

We are there.

With every second you have,

With your entire journey you have,

We are there.

We are always there... every step of the

way, with all of our love... we are there

CHAPTER 10
Our Facebook Group

I would like to acknowledge a special group of amazing administrators from our Facebook Group – Signs From Your Loved Ones. Without their caring, loving, kindness, and volunteering their time, our group would not be where it is today. I thank you with all of my heart:

Claire Ann Stevenson, Saranji Bailey, Cindy Udd, Vijayabanu Chandramouli, Michelle Sultemeier, Hilda Garcia, Adele Motlow, Ruth Turpin Feldmeier, Renee Gaudreau Blazejewski, Lyn Ragan, Julie Ann Jade, Tammy Snook, Diana Lovering Brown, Samuel Stevenson, Breana Ashleigh, Mary Jane Yardley Greenlee, Mary Hudson, Linda Lavelle, Lynn LaRose, Leza Poliakova, Linda B. Giordano, James T. Kochevar, Tina Louise Pielstick.

Claire Ann Stevenson has been with our group nearly from the very start, only a few weeks after I created our group, Claire was already busy from the start helping members with her comforting comments, inspirational poems, and quotes she shares every single day. After a couple of months, our group was growing faster than I could keep up with on my own, as I was also working a full-time day job. To help our group to keep running smoothly and to keep up with so many members asking to be added to join our group I started thinking, I needed to add an administrator to help me.

I did not even really know Claire except I knew she'd lost her son, Graham. Since Claire's name kept popping into my head, I took it as a sign that I was meant to ask her if she would like to help our group as an administrator. She said yes and continues to work very hard for all of us. I have asked Claire to share her story and experience in the next couple of pages.

In the months and years after adding Claire as an administrator, we now have an excellent group of very kind, caring, compassionate, loving members of our group as administrators, all volunteering their time and experience to help, guide, bring some comfort, healing and a piece of mind to those who have to deal with the loss/crossing over of a loved one, for which I am so very thankful for they are doing to help make our group what it has become today to over at this writing to over 163,000 members. Thank you.

Our Facebook Group

On our group page on Signs From Our Loved Ones –
https://www.facebook.com/groups/SignsFromOur – we
have a set of guidelines to keep our group in a very
positive and loving place to share what we are all going
through, our loss, grief, heartbreak, loneliness, emotions,
pain and everything that goes along with having to deal
with the loss/crossing over of a loved one; to know we
are not alone with all that we are going through, to know
we are not going crazy and to know what we are going
through is what all those who are grieving are going
through. We do all grieve differently and in our own
way, but many of the emotions and feelings are the same
and it's something we are all or have all been dealing with
the loss/crossing over of our loved ones. We have a great
group of administrators who all volunteer their time and
energy to help our group to always be a very safe and
positive place for everyone to share about their
loss/crossing over of a loved ones, to help learn and teach
from their own experiences and learn from others. We
also have a great group of people on both Signs From
Our Loved Ones group who also help, learn, teach one
another that they are not alone with all they are going
through and to know our loved ones are still so very
much around us for which I am so very thankful for all of
their help, kindness, and love.

Our group is a place where we are able to share our experiences to know we are not the only ones who are feeling or experiencing these emotions. It's a place where we are able to help and learn from one another and bring some comfort and healing, one small step and one day at a time. To help gain some knowledge from one another that grieving is a very slow process, and if need be taken at one moment, to one minute, to one hour, to one day at a time. We will never "get over it." We learn to do the best we can, one day at a time, at our own pace, done our way and to know we will always grieve for the loss/crossing over of our loved ones and at the same time we know with time our loved ones want us to be happy and to live our lives to the fullest, which bring them great joy to see.

Members are able to read the many posting and their comments from our many members who help and learn from one another, share their comments and postings. It's okay to join our group and just read some of the many postings by our members, if you feel comfortable just reading postings and comments, that's okay and with time if you ever feel comfortable sharing, please feel free, it's always your choice. We have a number of members who just read our many postings; if this brings them comfort and healing… great. Even if you never post a comment or posting, with time by what you have learned, it helps you in your healing process and you may help others around you in a time of their loss. We all help each other in some way and that is what it's all about.

To go along with our members sharing their many experiences through postings and comments, we also share many inspiring quotes, messages, songs, and helpful resources to help bring some comfort, healing and a peace of mind.

The second part of our group is exactly what the title of the group is… sharing the countless different ways our loved ones are able to send us to get our attention they are still so very much around us, a great help to bring some comfort, healing and a peace of mind. Our members help and learn from one another by sharing the many different ways we receive signs from our loved ones, helping us be more aware of the many ways our loved ones try to let us know they are still very much with us and all of their love. The more people who share their experiences, the more others will start to share and the more open we all become to understanding that our loved ones can and do send us signs they are still so very much around us with all of their love.

With so many people joining our group and with some members who feel more comfortable sharing within a closed or private group, I created a second group called Signs From Our Loved Ones–2. https://www.facebook.com/groups/249249048540255/ It's the same as our public group, but only the members are able to see and read the postings/comments. Some members are in both groups, sharing what they feel comfortable posting on our public group and keep other postings and comment they feel more comfortable with our closed group. All are welcome to feel free to visit or join our group whenever you like.

Members not only share what they are going through, their grieving, pain, depression, fears, loss, heartbreak, and much more they help and learn from one another., Members also share inspirational songs on our group page, articles, websites, videos, radio or TV programs, and more helpful resources to bring comfort and peace of mind to one another.

Now, in her own words, our administrator:

Claire Ann Stevenson

The world as I knew it came to a sudden tragic end with an early morning phone call September 22, 2007. I learned that my treasured twenty–two–year–old son, Graham, was dead.

He died in a freak accidental fall as he was walking across a highway bridge on his way back to his apartment in the early morning hours.

Graham had just started his senior year of college. He had a scholarship in Art and was a gifted Graphic Design major. He had amazing artistic vision. Graham was full of thoughts and ideas with plans for his future following his upcoming graduation. We were all anticipating what he would do.

The shock and anguish of having a child pass goes beyond words. In a moment, a huge purpose and focus in my life was gone. It was almost paralyzing. Graham's death propelled me into a desperate search for meaning and purpose. I read many books on grief and spirituality. I started taking yoga classes. I attended grief groups and Afterlife Awareness conferences. I listened to radio shows on many metaphysical subjects. Most importantly, I started a daily practice of meditation.

I yearned to connect with my son. The longing of my heart was answered. A year and a half after Graham died, poetry started coming to me. It was a miraculous healing gift of love from across dimensions. The poems turned into a book called, "A Mother's Tears – Poems of Heartbreak, Loss, and Discovery."

Four years after Graham's passing, a friend of mine from a grief group told me about a Facebook group I should check out. It was *Guy Dusseault's* Signs From Our Loved Ones.

At that time, I did very little on the computer and didn't belong to any online groups. My friend had joined Guy's group and thought I would like it, too. She encouraged me to join, so I did. This was in December 2011, a month after the group was created.

I believe there were around 200 members when I joined. I shared with the group some of my poems and photos and stories of signs I felt that I was receiving from my son.

It is truly amazing. There is a hunger for a unique group like this. It is so much more than grief support. Signs From Our Loved Ones *gives so much comfort and hope in teaching us that love never ends. We don't have to wait until we pass to be with our loved ones in spirit. They are with us still and show us this in many ways.*

There is nothing more comforting to me than understanding we are eternally connected and our relationships are ongoing. I spend full-time hours working with both of these online groups. It helps me to feel I am helping others who are grieving by spreading this important message.

I don't believe a friend encouraging me to join this group or Guy asking me to be an administrator were random events. I believe there is a greater plan at work.

There is so much we don't consciously know. I have been learning to walk in faith and to listen to my heart.

There is no greater power than love. It transcends space and time.

I know my son walks with me.

CHAPTER 11
Inspirational Poems

These next few pages, I wanted to share a few of the inspirational quotes and poems some of our members have created and are sharing and being shared by others on our group.

A special thank you to Lyn Ragan, Cindy Adkins, Cindy Udd, Kendell Buckley, Constance Economos, Julie Ann Jade, Jo Jo Lachapelle, Claire Ann Stevenson, Lorraine Nicholls, Jean Dudley Johnson, and Christina Mahaney for allowing me to share their inspirational poems and quotes with all of you.

Poems

The storm will always be there... it is weaker and I have strengthened
I will always hear the rumble of grief, but the sound is

distant from yesterday. I will continue to feel the wave of rainfall from my eyes, but it doesn't pour like it did in the past. This storm will continue to weaken but it will strengthen the memory of your amazing smile and the strong love that we shared. These memories will forever warm my heart until it beats no more.

—*Written by Constance Economos*

~ ~ ~ ~ ~

I talk to you every morning
I talk to you every night,
A silent conversation between you and I
I know you hear me at times,
I think I hear you too,
I look for you like children
I pretend it's hide and seek
I see a shadow or so I think
From the corner of my eye
I feel you right behind me
You are always at my side
I talk to you

—*Written by Julie Ann Jade*

~ ~ ~ ~ ~

I am not gone, I am not gone
How could that be, Love is eternal
That means eternity
I'm just gone from your vision
I'm not gone from your heart that which is eternal cannot
be ripped apart
Grieve not for my passing it does not mean the end
For love and life is eternal
evolving, unbreakable, unending
my sweet and loving friend hold on to my memory
For in your heart I'm free
Until the day we meet again
Your love still lives in me.

—Written by Jo Jo Lachapelle

~ ~ ~ ~ ~

Never Say Goodbye

Those we love are never gone. The bonds of love ate
much too strong, always only a thought away, within our
hearts you will stay.

The physical body wasn't you, your eternal essence is
what is true, the earthly form has only changes,
transitioning to heavenly gain.

One with God, and peace, blessed the sweet release, we
can't help mourn for what we miss, But we'll take

comfort in knowing this.

Thank you for all our years of sharing, the memories of love and caring, Emotions are hard, and though we cry, we never really say good–bye.

http://amotherstears.blogspot.com/

~ ~ ~ ~ ~

Are you somewhere over the rainbow or deep down below the sea?

Are you shining with the twinkling stars, too far for me to see?

Are you the gentle breeze, gently blowing on my face?

Are you a fluffy cloud in some happy faraway place?

I wonder why I can't see or hear you, you are so far away from me

But I know there are places where I am sure you will be.

You will be in the tears we shed for you every single day,

Memories of you with us, at work or rest or play

I feel you in every hug, every kiss or gentle touch

I see you in every room at home, but miss holding you so much

I feel you in each heartbeat, I see you in your sister's eyes,

You are in our thoughts daily from sunset to sunrise.

I know you are the shadow, staying oh so close to me,

I swear I felt you touch my face, it felt so very real

I see you in your dad the man you should have grown to be,

and reminders of you emerge in your nephews and niece,

Although these walls are filled with grief and are lacking of your sound

I know through signs you have sent me that you are still around

In our smiles, our souls, our hearts, the essence of you lives on.

And I know with every passing day we will be re-united son.

In memory of our son Daniel Scruba Nicholls

—*By Lorraine Nicholls*

~ ~ ~ ~ ~

In honor of our son, Liam

He was my heart, without him here my heart beats broken.

He was my air, without him I cannot breathe.

He was my life, without him I wonder if it's worth living.

You read these words, and they are only words to you.

But they are my thoughts, my feelings... my life.

There's an emptiness you could not fathom.

There is a type of grief beyond explanation.

To lose a child is like having lost a major organ in your body.

A part of you is suddenly gone with no warning, no goodbyes, no explanation.

The pain is agonizing.

Every beat of your heart is painful.

Every breath is like gasping for air.

Every child you see suddenly becomes the child you lost.

You grieve wondering what would he be doing right now?

You suddenly see life in a new form, every rainbow represents their smile, every butterfly is a sign from them.

You notice things you hadn't before, the beautiful sunset in the horizon.

The clouds how they look like angel wings.

Everything has changed everything is different.

You don't even recognize yourself anymore.

You worry more, you sleep less. You can smile but you can also cry a river of tears.

One minute you think maybe things will be okay but the next moment you're not sure how you ever felt that way, and it feels like your life is falling apart all over again. This is what it feels like to be a grieving parent.

You no longer have control over your feelings. You realize you have no control over your life. The sense of vulnerability you feel is unfair that any person should have to feel this way.

You never imagined in your life you could miss somebody so much and feel so dead when in fact you're so alive. It's the price we pay for love and as much as I hurt today I would have Liam all over again even if I knew how it ended, because the five years I had with him were the happiest of my life.

He was my reason, without him here I'm trying to find mine.

God bless you Liam mommy loves and misses you so much.

—*By Christina Mahaney 2016*

~ ~ ~ ~ ~

I'll never be truly happy and complete with you gone, I haven't seen you is so long.

So long I forgot your scent

But I have to be content with the photos left behind, it's like a little shrine.

They remind me of the good time,

My heart stops when I think of you

This emptiness never ceases too

The love I have for you my brother is like no other

I feel your protecting me like a cover

From down under I look up to you like I did as a child,

we were wild

None of this was mild, but I put on a smile

Momma needed me, strong, for so long

I never got to grieve but no need for me

One day we will meet again and pretend that none of this ever happened

Like it was all a dream and I'll finally figure out what life really means

Until we meet again my best friend, see you then.

—*By Kendell Buckley, in honor of her brother*

~ ~ ~ ~ ~

Forever By Our Side

You've climbed that highest mountain, Your earthly life is done, You are home again in heaven, All your battles here won.

Some people live a lot of years, others only a few, Many lives are only minutes, Just briefly passing through.

What is the rhyme or reason? We desperately want to know, Our hearts are torn and aching, Not wanting ever to let go.

Parents never think to bury their children, Our minds don't work that way, We assume our children will remain here, Long after we've passed away.

The shock and trauma of your child dying, Is a pain

beyond this earth, Parents promise to love and care for, Their children from their birth.

Although we no longer see our children, Or hear their voice, They are a part of us forever, In this we can rejoice.

Love is not the body, Love does not die, We miss their presence, But know our children stay close by.

We feel them with us always, Their love is now our guide, We are blessed to have them with us, Forever by our sides.

—*Written by Claire Ann Stevenson*

~ ~ ~ ~ ~

No Time Limit On Grief

Just because you think I've grieved too long, my friend,
Please do not bring a hasty end
To my remarks if they speak of loss
Because talking about my loved one is the cost
Of healing. I just must express
The pain I felt the day she left.
I need to talk about her ways,
About my lengthening lonely days
Since she's been gone.
Talking like this helps along
My healing. So many people say it's true,

But when I try to talk to you
About my pain, you cut me short,
Change the topic, rush to abort
Whatever I was planning to say,
Maybe wanting, instead, to stay gay
In a world where the realities are sometimes sad,
Where people mourn what they once had.
So if you prefer to pretend all is right,
Don't ask me how I'm doing, because it might
Start an onslaught of speech and tears from me,
Something uncomfortable for you to see.
Do not put a timer on my grief.
Do not tell me I should not release
Tears o'er her at this late date.
You'll understand someday. Just wait.
Grief can last for periods long,
And there is certainly nothing wrong
With feeling tears at the oddest time.
So talk with me when I'm feeling low.
Don't turn away and move to go,
Thinking I should be well
by now, because one can never tell
How long grief will stick around.
Just listening quietly I have found
Helps to ease my heart's breaking.
Bit by bit these steps I'm taking

Will move me forward, lessen grief,
So do not suddenly break free
If I start speaking through my tears
Of my loved one. Stay with me
And listen to me tenderly.
Do not say "buck up" or
"Just don't think about it"
Just because you feel inept
Comforting me doesn't mean to get
Tired of what I have to say,
Afraid it'll make you feel less gay.
Eventually, I hope the talks
Will help me to live with my loss
A little better, with a smaller hole
Than the one I now carry in my soul.

—By Jean Dudley Johnson

CHAPTER 12
Inspirational Quotes

I was supposed to spend the rest
Of my life with you
And then I realized… you spent the
Rest of your life with me.
I smile because I know you love me
Till the day you went away.
And will keep loving me…
Till the day we're together again.

By Lyn Ragan
Wake Me Up – Facebook page

~ ~ ~ ~ ~

Some people think
That grief is over in a
Month or even a year.
They have no idea that
It is a process that can
Only be experienced
One day at a time.

By Lyn Ragan
Wake Me Up – Facebook page

~ ~ ~ ~ ~

Everything can change in the blink
Of an eye. Appreciate those you love,
Forgive often, and hug frequently.

By Lyn Ragan

~ ~ ~ ~ ~

When you died,
I died with you
My heart stopped, my mind went
Into shock, and my thoughts
Became a one−way ticket to you.
I asked you a hundred times a day,
"How do I do this without you?"
And then you changed everything.
You started to show me signs of your
Survival and proved to me how alive
You really are.

By Lyn Ragan
Wake Me Up − Facebook page.

~ ~ ~ ~ ~

One day, I'll meet you
On the other side
I know you'll be standing there
With your arms open wide
I'll tell you how it's been
Without you here
But then, it won't matter
Because you'll finally be near.
I'll see your smile that
Could light up a room
And tell you how I wished
You weren't gone so soon.
We'll hold each other tight
Right in front of heaven's gate
I'll look at you with love
As you have always been my fate

By Cindy Adkins
Facebook –Angels at My Door

~ ~ ~ ~ ~

No matter where you
Are, you will
Always be inside
My heart.
Time and distance

And even death
Can never keep our
Spirits apart.

By Cindy Adkins
Facebook page – Angels At My Door.

~ ~ ~ ~ ~

Signs

Signs from loved ones
Are a blessing, indeed
They seem to appear
In your hour of need.
You may not realize it
But your angels are around
When you least expect signs
They seem to be found.
You miss your special angels
And wish they were here
But there is comfort in
Knowing that they are always near.

By Cindy Adkins
Facebook page – Angels At My Door

~ ~ ~ ~ ~

Hugs From Your Loved Ones

What is a spiritual hug

A wonderful tingling sensation that travels

From one end of your body to the other.

Sometimes just a touching feeling

It is a comfort and makes you feel

Good even if you are beyond sad

Your facial muscles begin to relax

A peace surrounds your being

You find yourself suddenly smiling

Embrace this experience

As you are being hugged

From a loved one above

By Cindy Udd
Facebook page − Soul Healing

~ ~ ~ ~ ~

When someone leaves this world

That we love with all of our heart

Grief hits us like an immense tidal wave

Drowning in the tears that seem to never end.

Please know that in time, the waves of tears

Do become further apart and less frequent.

Eventually all begins to become almost smooth

Life is never the same, but yes we can laugh and live

Until it is our time to re−unite with our loved ones.

By Cindy Udd
Facebook page − Soul Healing

~ ~ ~ ~ ~

Feel free to visit or join our group page, Signs From Our Loved, or closed group, Signs From Our loved Ones−2. You don't have to post anything. Just read some of our many postings by our wonderful members who are all here for the same reason, helping, learning, guiding, comforting and to give each other a peace of mind to know that we are not along.

Thank you,
Guy Dusseault

CHAPTER 13
Helpful Resources

Suicide Hotline Information

Grieving for the loss of a loved one causes great anxiety and panic for many of us who are grieving and can also at times cause some people to think about suicide. Please, if you are having these thoughts or feelings please call the suicide hotline for help.

National Suicide Prevention Hotline: **800–273–8255**

Website: www.suicideprenventionlifeline.org

Worldwide Suicide Prevention Website:
www.suicide.org/international–suicide–hotlines.html

Please know that our loved ones who are still with us want with all of their hearts to keep living. It's the same for all of our loved ones who have crossed over to heaven. They want for us to continue to live and to follow our own journey and to know they are by our side to help and guide us along the way with all of their love. Please take care and God Bless.

Helpful Books

Here is a list of helpful books read by some of our members. To learn more about many of these books, you can visit the page/websites of the authors or any of the online retailers (Amazon, Barnes & Noble, iTunes, Google Play, etc.)

A Mother's Tears by Claire Ann Stevenson

Hello from Heaven by Bill Guggenheim

Gone too Soon by Jon Baer (for dads)

Visits from Heaven by Josie Varga

The Afterlife of Billy Fingers by Annie Kagen

We Don't Die by George Anderson

Walking in the Garden of Souls by George Anderson

Heaven & Earth by James Van Praagh

Healing Grief by James Van Praagh

Growing up in Heaven by James Van Praagh

Ghost Among Us by James Van Praagh

Proof of Heaven by Eben Alexander

We are Eternal by Robert Brown

Power of the Soul by John Holland

Soul Shift by Mark Ireland

Signs From Above by Doreen Virtue

Embraced by the Light by Betty Eadie

Many Lives Many Masters by Brian Weiss

Closer to the Light by Melvin Morse, M.D.

Life After Life by Richard Moody, M.D.

Saved by the Light & Peace in the Light by Dannion Brinkley

Understanding Spirit Understanding Yourself by Vicki Monroe

Transforming Fate Into Destiny by Robert Ohotto

Extraordinary Experiences that Changed Lives by Dan Millman and Doug Childers

The Last Frontier Exploring the Afterlife and Transforming our Fears of Death by Julie Assante

The Gift of Grief by Matthew Gewirtz

Never Letting Go by Mark Anthony

Tear Soup by Scheibert and DeKlyen

We Need to Talk by Lyn Ragan

Wake Me Up by Lyn Ragan

He Blew Her a Kiss by Angie Pechak Printup

Children of the Dome by Rosemary Smith

Closer Than you Think by Deborah Heneghan

The Shack by Wm. Paul Young

The Sunroom by Beverly Lewis

Don't Sweat the Small Stuff by Richard Carlson, Ph.D.

When God Winks at You by Squire Rushnell

No Regrets My Love by Margaret Cowie

The Widowbago Tour by Margaret Cowie

Travel Guide from Heaven by Anthony DeStefano

The Gift Giver by Jennifer Hawkins

Footprints in the Sand by Laura Tomei

Angel Miracles by Cindy Adkins

Forever With You by Patrick Matthews

I'll Be the Brightest Star by Arlene Ricciardi Tellis

A Breath Away by Lynda Matthews

Between 2 Worlds by Isabella Hunt

A Bridge to Healing: J.T's Story by Sarah Baptista

Grieving Dads: To the Brink and Back by Kelly Farley

The Angel in My Pocket by Sukey Forbes

Listen Up, The Other Side is Talking by Kelle Sutliff

Second First by Christina Rasmussen

Mum Moments, Journey Through Grief by Judy Taylor

Dreaming Kevin by Carla Blowey

Hitting Fear Head On by Laurie Moon—Boggs

18 Stepping Stones to Transforming Grief by Laurie Moon—Boggs

A Glimpse of Heaven, Heavenly Hugs, One Last Hug Before I Go by Carla Wills—Brandon

Rainbows, Butterflies & One Last Hug by Peggy S. Imm—Anesi

A Mothers LOSS 1 & 2 by Annie Mithcell

Signs from the Afterlife by Lyn Ragan

Kim: A Dying Child's Spiritual Legacy by Fred G Womack

No Ordinary Coincidence by Donna Salyers

The Complete Idiot's Guide to Communicating with Spirits by Rita S. Berkowitz

Chicken Soup for the Soul by Jack Canfield

~ ~ ~ ~ ~

Helpful Websites and Groups

www.oursonbilly.com

www.signsfromourlovedones.com

http://www.facebook.com/groups/SignsFromOurLoved
Ones/

https://www.facebook.com/groups/249249048540255/
Signs from our loved ones—2

http://www.cindyadkinsbooks.com/

https://www.facebook.com/groups/256369014386004/
Visits from Heaven

http://www.childrenofdome.com/

http://www.spacebetweenbreaths.com/

http://www.thelightbeyond.com/

http://www.soulkisses.com/

http://www.facebook.com/AngelsAtMyDoor

http://www.connect.legacy.com/

http://www.heartlightstudios.net/

http://www.facebook.com/pages/Death—of—a—Loved—
one—Quotes—Poems—and—Resources/310515538965543

http://www.theworstclubintheworld.org/

http://www.facebook.com/grieftoolbox

http://www.virtual-memorials.com/

http://www.wisdom-of-spirit.com/

http://www.signsfromourlovedones.wordpress.com/

http://www.vickimonroe.com

https://www.facebook.com/groups/77733417608/

Never Letting Go

https://www.facebook.com/groups/griefunspoken/

https://www.facebook.com/groups/1459056241014900/

Soul Healing

https://www.facebook.com/groups/interlife/

https://www.facebook.com/groups/ChildrenShouldntDieFirst/

https://www.facebook.com/AngelsAtMyDoor/photos/a.430141760340105.92838.430141097006838/923436994343910/?type=1

https://www.facebook.com/groups/175181872562202/

https://www.facebook.com/griefcoach/

https://www.pamelamarieedmunds.com

https://www.facebook.com/pages/Leslie-Dutton-Medium/429331027143110

http://www.jenniferavalon.net

https://www.facebook.com/groups/891641840885287/
Renee Blazejewski–Reiki Healer & Spiritual medium

https://www.facebook.com/june.evans.5283

https://www.facebook.com/saranji.bailey
https://www.facebook.com/groups/1459056241014900/
Cindy Udd Soul Healing

CHAPTER 14
Acknowledgments

I want to thank every single person and all of our loved ones who have crossed over, our spirit guides, angels, and God with all of my heart for all of the help and guidance, to put this inspirational and comforting book of information together.

I have too many names to acknowledge, a number of them are mentioned throughout the book. Without everyone's help, guidance, insight, experiences, and the endless questions I have asked, I would not have been able to put this book together.

I want to give a very special thank you and send hugs to all the amazing administrators on our two Signs From Our Loved Ones Facebook group pages who I am honored to call my friends. Without their amazing love, kindness, and volunteering their time while grieving themselves, our group would not be where it is: a very supportive, loving, caring, helpful, comforting place to share about their loss/crossing over of a loved one and to know they are not alone with all they are going through, and to know our loved ones are still so very much by our side with all of their love for us.

I also want to thank all of our members for taking the time to share their own experiences, sharing, helping, comforting one another with all of their postings and comments, to know we are all here on our group to help and learn from on another that we are not alone... Thank you.

A very special thank you to my wife, Jo−Anne, love you.

Thank you to our son Robert, love you.

Also, to our son, Billy, who crossed over on June 26, 2004, for all of his help and guidance with all we are doing. Love you, Billy, and thank you.

Thank you to all of my family and friends.

Always remember, to our loved ones who have crossed over, it is all about the love. Love is everything.

God Bless!

ABOUT THE AUTHOR

 Guy Dusseault is husband to Jo-Anne and father to two sons, Bill and Robert. After to loss and crossing over of their son, Billy, as they called him.

Guy started researching about connecting with his son eight months after he crossed over. Guy and Jo-Anne had a reading with spirit medium, Vicki Monroe, which opened up Guy's connection with Billy in different ways. Billy's favorite means of communicating signs are the moon, lights, and clouds all taking the shape of hearts, just like the one on the cover.

In 2005, Guy created the website _www.oursonbilly.com_ in honor of Billy to help his family heal and also to help others know they are not alone when they are dealing with the loss of a loved one.

Guy has done several radio shows with Pamela Marie Edmunds' Bridges Between Two Worlds, Christopher Reburn, and Vicki Monroe, to name a few. He loves to share his story of his loss and the ways he has been able to see the signs his son sends to them.

He has a blog called *Signs from Our Loved Ones*: https://signsfromourlovedones.wordpress.com/ and later added a second website www.signsfromourlovedones.com which is about the different signs our loved ones are able to send us.

In November 2011, Guy created a Facebook group called *Signs from Our Loved Ones* as a way of reaching people from all over the world to let them know they are not alone with everything they are going through with the loss/crossing over of a loved one and the many different ways our loved ones are able to connect with us. The group is a safe, positive, loving place for everyone to help, learn, and bring comfort and healing to one another.

Guy's story has also been in several books including *Visits from Heaven* by Josie Varga, *He Blew Her a Kiss* by Angie Printup and Kelly Stewart Dollar, and *Signs from the Afterlife* by Lyn Ragan.

Guy works daily on his Facebook groups with the help of a great bunch of administrators who donate their time to support the members who all help one another to know we are not alone.

www.oursonbilly.com
info@oursonbilly.com

17768869R00069

Printed in Poland
by Amazon Fulfillment
Poland Sp. z o.o., Wrocław